Solar
Cooking
Adventures

by
Jackass Jill

Solar Cooking Adventures

Introduction

A few years ago I looked around my comfortable campsite and noticed the solar battery charger for my cell phone and laptop, another solar charger for assorted small batteries, a solar radio, solar lights, solar-powered gold wheel for prospecting—solar, solar, solar. The only thing missing was a solar oven!

Most of my life I cooked on wood stoves and campfires, until I noticed increasing breathing problems; on a few occasions I had to be hospitalized. I was allergic to smoke. I tried using unleaded gas for cooking, but it gave me headaches and the gas jostling around in panniers often leaked all over everything. Then I got the donkeys to carry heavy propane bottles to remote camp sites. Yuk.

Instead of hauling those heavy fuel tanks into roadless regions, the donkeys (Shaggy and Willy) now carry portable solar ovens, a single burner stove, and small propane bottles for early morning coffee and after-dark tea.

In southern New Mexico I can bake food in my solar ovens just about any day of the year. Lots of food: Squash bread, pumpkin bread, oatmeal bread, cinnamon raisin bread, fruit and nut squares, chicken casserole, lasagna, meat loaf, tuna loaf, baked beans, cornbread, and slumgullion stew. On the Olympic Peninsula in Washington state where I spend my summers (when I can) I also do some solar cooking—I could fill a book. In fact, that's exactly what I'm doing.

Types of Solar Ovens

I spent a few years experimenting with different types of solar ovens—from the foil covered pizza box variety, and conical reflector ovens, to solar box ovens with and without reflectors.

Now I have five solar cookers: one box oven size, and four fold-up backpack sizes. One is a windshield shade solar cooker.

A simple pizza-box style oven. This type oven will heat food and keep your coffee warm, but it isn't as efficient as the conical fold-up versions.

Because I have two large donkeys, Shaggy and Willy, to pack all my gear, I can bring to my campsites such luxuries as a cot, thick foam pad, gear and equipment tent, a large sleeping tent, mining tools, lots of food, coffee, tea, wine, pots and pans, cooler, water purifier, propane stove and small propane bottles, and a decent size solar box oven. The amount of stuff I can carry with two donkeys is about the same as an SUV can haul to a campsite.

My pack donkeys, Shaggy in front, and Willy in back.

If I were backpacking and did not want to hire a Sherpa, I'd take a fold-up cardboard type reflector oven, with a black, light-weight roasting pan, and turkey roasting bags. The roasting bags act as a solar heat collector when you're not using a box oven.

The reason for black pots and pans is the black absorbs the heat, then the heat gets trapped in the cooking bag or oven and raises the temperature in the cooking area. These black pots or roasters all need lids to keep the moisture in and for faster cooking, except when baking bread.

Solar oven with two, 3-quart size, black cooking pots.

For areas with limited water, or in my case not
wanting to scrub out pots, I bring lots of aluminum
foil or lots of parchment paper. I line each cooking
pot with foil or paper.

Turkey-type roasting bags (available in any supermarket) are a necessity when cooking in these open-style reflector ovens.

Cardboard-backed solar reflective oven. This type of oven is my favorite travel oven. It folds down to the size of a double-issue magazine.

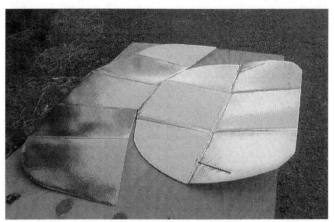

Flattened out solar oven.

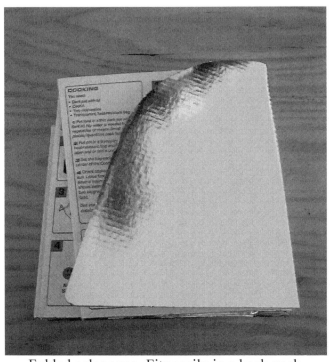

Folded solar oven. Fits easily in a back pack.

A complete two pot-size solar oven folded up under
a 3-quart cooking pot.

This solar oven is available through Solar Cookers
International.

Use some type of spacer, like wood or flat stones, under the cooking pots for cardboard or any non-metal solar cooker.

My second favorite solar cooker is this solar funnel cooker made from an auto sun shade that you can purchase at any hardware or auto parts store for $5 to $10.

You fashion this reflective accordion fold-up car sunshade into a funnel shape and set it over a five-gallon bucket. Use clothes-pins or clips to secure it to the top of the bucket, put a cookie sheet, cake rack or whatever over the bucket hole so your cooking pot doesn't fall through, then place your black cooking pot filled with uncooked goodies in a turkey roasting bag, set the cooking bag and pot on the rack over the five-gallon bucket, and face the funnel cooker toward the sun. Then go read or take a hike, and in a few hours your meal is ready in your solar crock-pot. The windshield shade also doubles as an emergency blanket in your vehicle and in the backcountry.

This solar funnel cooker wasn't my idea. I got the details from: www.solarcooking.org/plans/windshield-cooker.htm. (Their funnel cooker looks better than mine because they attached Velcro and placed a stick across the widest part of the funnel to keep it spread out and to stop it from flopping over in the wind.)

This is a box type solar oven. Because it is enclosed, you don't need to use the turkey roasting bags. This model oven has a clear plastic, double-paned lid, and is shown without the attachable reflectors. During the summers in the Southwest I did not need the reflectors. This type of oven gets hotter and cooks faster than the open type solar ovens.

Solar oven with reflector

I use this oven with the detachable reflectors during the winter months and on cloudy days. It is a good idea to remove the reflectors on windy days, or move the oven out of the wind. Notice that behind the cooking pots is an oven thermometer—a good thing to have. This oven is called the SOS (Solar Oven Society) Sport.

All the ovens and cooking pots I use are available through www.solarcookers.org. Solar Cookers International. SCI sells kits, cookbooks, and the Global Sun Oven, a very efficient solar cooker, though more expensive than the Sport. This organization also has plans for building your own ovens.

A permanent "through-the-wall" plywood box
cooker by Barbara Kerr. See
www.solarcooking.org/bkerr/DoItYourself.htm

Basic rice.

Basic Rice

1 cup organic long grain brown rice
(or your favorite rice)
2 ½ cups broth or water
½ to 1 teaspoon salt
or 2 tablespoons soy sauce
1-2 teaspoons butter
or your favorite oil
Cover, and leave in your
solar cooker 2-4 hours.
Length of time depends on your
solar oven and time of year.

Solar cooked rice and cornbread.

Basic Cornbread

(Buy a cornbread mix and follow
instructions)
or
1 cup whole wheat
or white flour
1 cup cornmeal
2 teaspoons baking powder
½ teaspoon salt
Mix the dry ingredients
Then mix together 2 eggs
1 cup milk
Up to a ½ cup of honey
or ¾ cup sugar
½ cup oil or melted butter
Add the mixed, wet ingredients
to the dry ingredients
Cover and cook in solar oven
for 1 ½ to 3 hours

Precautions

Sometimes I forget how hot these innocent looking cookers can get, and have grabbed a pot of stew with my bare hands. Ouch! USE GLOVES OR SOME TYPE OF INSULATION TO MOVE POT! A pair of socks (preferably clean) work well as oven mitts.

When using reflector-type ovens; DON'T FORGET TO WEAR SUNGLASSES. Use the same eye protection as you would when boating or snow skiing on a sunny day.

In this book I won't deal with the bowl shaped parabolic solar cookers the size of commercial satellite dishes. They are used in China to feed large groups of people and require welding-type eye protection, and singe the hair right off your arms. You can't turn your back on these parabolic cookers or your meal will burn.

Solar Cooking Adventures

My recipes and cooking instructions are for slow, low heat (225-300 degrees) cookers that you can safely leave all day like a crock-pot. Your food will never burn and will stay moist.

Tips: Place your oven on a flat, stable surface. The tailgate of a pick-up truck or SUV works well. Face your oven toward the sun. Reposition it every few hours for full sun and faster cooking. If you'll be gone most the day, turn the oven a few degrees west, to face what will be the sun's position in 2 or 3 hours.

Repeat: The reason for black cooking pots is the black absorbs the heat. By placing your cooking pot into a roasting bag, the heat gets trapped in the cooking bag and raises the temperature in the cooking area. These black pots or roasters all need lids to keep the moisture in and for faster cooking, except when baking bread.

The roasting bags (buy the large turkey size) act as a solar heat collector when you're using fold up type reflector ovens. You don't need to use roasting bags in totally enclosed solar box ovens.

Cooking times also vary depending on your solar cooker and where you live. A foil covered pizza box type oven doesn't get as hot as a conical reflector oven. Some solar box ovens with reflectors can reach 325 degrees in the fall and 350 without reflectors in the summer.

Note: When I first started using solar ovens, I kept opening the cooking bags or lids to peek. This lets out all the heat and can double the actual cooking time. Now I generally don't peek for at least an hour or two. And if you wander off and forget to check (even better) your meal will be fine. Solar cooking is much like using a crock-pot, except you use less water, thus reducing the cooking time.

The dogs, cats, donkeys, my camping buddy, Texas Jack, and I, all eat well. Problem is when camping, with no fridge or freezer, we feel the need to eat everything as it comes freshly baked from the ovens.

The last picture I saw of myself from the back while I was packing one of my donkeys was hilarious—way too big for my britches. This reminded me of a quote from Jill Charlotte Stanford's *The Cowgirl's Cookbook*, "Sometimes we just have to put on our 'Big Girl Britches' and deal with it!"

So no more big butt recipes for us. Texas Jack was not excited about this change of fare, but he had, I noted, developed a too-many-desserts gut and man boobs. Joey the dog, now in his middle age, was sporting a wide load. So I began working on the solar cooking chapters: Skinny Ass Cooking, Wild Ass Cooking, and Smart Ass Guide to Solar Food Drying & Water Purifying.

While eating pigeon breasts (see Wild Ass Cooking section) and celery sticks one evening we fantasized about the last dessert recipe I made in the solar oven, I called it the **Gold Diggers Cake:1 yellow cake mix, 4 eggs, ¾ cup oil or softened**

butter, 1 cup water. Mix these together, then add one can of your favorite frosting (coconut pecan is good) and mix. Put into a covered skillet or 3-quart pot, and place in your preheated solar oven for 1-2 hours on a hot sun day. (See this recipe in the Sweet Ass Cooking section.)

Another recipe that brings back fond memories is what I call my **Braying Burro Biscuits, actually a simple cinnamon apple crisp** named after my pack donkey, Shaggy. When he smelled the apple crisp cooking he would bray a series of long pitiful brays until the apple crisp was cool enough for him to eat. (This recipe is in the Sweet Ass Cooking section.)

Tomorrow I'll try some Skinny Ass recipes with lots of healthy vegetables…maybe.

Texas Jack in camp.

SKINNY ASS COOKING
(Low Fat and Vegetarian)

Beef Taco Bean Soup

2 lbs rump roast cut into bite-sized pieces
1 package taco seasoning
1 (15 oz) can Mexican style diced tomatoes,
or salsa
1 small can green chilies
1 can tomato sauce (8 oz.)
1 onion, chopped
2 beef bouillon cubes
2 cans red kidney beans,
(15 oz. each), rinsed, drained
Shredded cheddar cheese
Roll the cut meat in taco seasoning
and add to pot.
Then add the tomatoes, chilies, tomato sauce,
onion, and bouillon cubes.
Cover and place in solar oven for 3-4 hours
or until meat is tender.
Add the drained beans
and cook another 45 minutes.
Serve topped with cheese.
(You can also cook your own
pre-soaked beans for this recipe.
Put your rinsed and soaked uncooked
beans in the bottom of your pot,
cover with water (or water/broth combination),
one inch over top of beans.
Then add meat and the rest of ingredients
and cook for 6-8 hours.)

Adapted from the *Crock Pot Cookbook:*
440 Slow Cooker Recipes,
by Robert Wilson, Kindle eBook.

Cabbage and Beef Casserole

2 lbs ground beef
1 head cabbage, shredded
(I prefer red cabbage)
1 medium chopped onion
1 (16 oz.) can tomatoes
or same amount fresh tomatoes
Beef broth or tomato juice to cover
bottom of pot
Garlic salt, thyme, red pepper
and a bit of oregano
Layer cabbage, onion, spices
 meat, and garlic salt
Repeat layers ending with beef.
Top with tomatoes, undrained
 and a dusting of oregano
Cover and bake for 3-6 hours

Adapted from the *Crock Pot Cookbook:
440 Slow Cooker Recipes*,
by Robert Wilson, Kindle eBook.

Sage Infused Chicken Livers

1-2 lbs chicken livers, trimmed,
washed, and patted dry
2 tablespoons melted butter
½ teaspoon salt
1 teaspoon black pepper
½ to 1 cup chopped fresh sage leaves
In your lined cooking pot put in
1 tablespoon melted butter
Make a single layer of livers,
season with salt and pepper
Sprinkle 1/3 of the sage
on this first layer of livers
Add additional layer or layers,
seasoning and sprinkling on sage
Then drizzle 1 tablespoon
melted butter over the top layer
Cover your pot and
cook for about 2 hours
(If you are serving this dish over rice,
save some of the sage and mix with
the rice before serving)

This recipe yields a rich sauce,
and I almost placed it in the
Big Ass Cooking chapter.

Adapted from a recipe by
WKB Potts, III, SolarOvens.org

Vegetable Casserole

2 cups carrots, cut in strips
2 cups chopped celery
1 diced onion
1-2 diced garlic cloves
1/4 cup diced green pepper
1 pint tomato juice
4 cups green beans,
fresh or frozen (thawed)
1 teaspoon salt or soy sauce
and dash of pepper
3 tablespoons tapioca
1 tablespoon brown
or white sugar, or honey
2 tablespoons olive or sesame oil
Mix all ingredients together in pot
Cover and cook for 4-5 hours.

Adapted from the *Crock Pot Cookbook:*
440 Slow Cooker Recipes,
by Robert Wilson, Kindle eBook.

Eggplant Zucchini Stew

1 lb plum tomatoes chopped
1 eggplant in 1/2" pieces
2 medium-zucchini in 1/2" pieces
1 onion finely chopped
3 stalks celery, sliced
1/2 cup chopped parsley
2 tablespoons red wine vinegar
1 tablespoon brown sugar
1/4 cup raisins
1/4 cup tomato paste
1 teaspoon salt or soy sauce
1/2 teaspoon freshly ground
black pepper
3 tablespoons oil
1 can drained black olives (optional)
2 tablespoons capers (optional)
Combine all the ingredients into your
cooking pot.
Cover and cook for 4-6 hours.
Serve warm or cold.

Adapted from the *Crock Pot Cookbook:*
440 Slow Cooker Recipes,
by Robert Wilson, Kindle eBook.

39

Vegetarian Stuffed Peppers

2 large green bell peppers
2 large red bell peppers
1/2 cup white or brown rice
1 (15 ounce) can whole kernel corn,
drained, or 2 cups thawed frozen corn
1 small can sliced black olives, drained
3 chopped green onions
1/4 teaspoon seasoned salt
1/4 teaspoon garlic pepper
1 (14-15ounce) can diced tomatoes,
undrained, or same amount of salsa
1/3 cup dry red wine
1 small can tomato paste or ketchup
Slice tops off peppers and carefully
remove seeds and inner ribs
Remove stems from tops and
chop remaining pepper pieces
Stand the peppers upright in your
3-5 quart pot.
In a separate bowl, combine
chopped pepper tops,
rice, corn, olives, green onions, seasoned salt,
garlic pepper, and 1/4 cup tomatoes.
Mix well.

Stuff peppers with corn/rice mixture,
dividing evenly and packing lightly.
Mix remaining tomatoes and their liquid
with wine and tomato paste until well blended.
Pour over and around the peppers.
Cover and cook for 4-6 hours
or until rice is cooked

Adapted from the *Ultimate Crockpot Cookbook:
750 Slow Cooker Recipes*, by Althea Champlain,
a Smashbooks Kindle eBook

Paprika Veggie Soup

5 large carrots (cubed)
2 lbs cauliflower (cubed)
or 8 large potatoes (cubed)
5 large celery stalks (sliced)
2 large onions (sliced thin)
3 tablespoons paprika
Salt and pepper to taste
Curry (optional)
Put all the ingredients into
a 5-quart pot, or into two 3-quart pots,
add water or vegetable broth
to top of veggies.
Cover and cook for 4-6 hours.

Adapted from the *Ultimate Crockpot Cookbook: 750 Slow Cooker Recipes*, by Althea Champlain, a Smashbooks Kindle eBook

Lentil Soup

1 cup dry lentils, rinsed
1 cup chopped carrots
1 cup chopped celery
1 cup chopped onion
2 cloves garlic, minced
1/2 teaspoon dried basil, crushed
1/2 teaspoon dried oregano, crushed
1/4 teaspoon dried thyme, crushed
1 bay leaf
3 1/2 cups chicken broth or veggie broth
1 1/2 cups water
1 (14-15 ounce) can Italian-style
stewed tomatoes (use undrained)
1/4 cup snipped fresh parsley
2 tablespoons cider vinegar
In your pot place lentils
and all the ingredients.
Cover and cook for 4-6 hours.

Adapted from the *Ultimate Crockpot Cookbook:
750 Slow Cooker* Recipes, by Althea Champlain,
a Smashbooks Kindle eBook

Split Peas

½ package of rinsed split peas
1 onion
5 whole garlic cloves
4 carrots, diced
1 cup cauliflower
(or red potatoes), cubed
Dash of soy sauce or salt,
pepper to taste
1 chopped jalapeno
Dash of ground cloves
3 tablespoons oil or butter
Place all the above ingredients in your pot.
Add enough water to cover mixture.
Cover and leave in the oven for 3-5 hours
Serve chunky or mash to thick texture
and serve.

Adapted from www.TheSunWorks.com

Baked Squash or Pumpkin

Remove pulp and seeds from
squash or pumpkin
Cut in half or quarter enough squash
or pumpkin to fill the bottom half
of your pot
Face the halves or quarters upright
so you can season with either a
butter/honey/maple syrup mixture,
or a butter/salt/pepper mixture.
Cover and place in solar cooker
for 3-4 hours.

Corn-On-The-Cob
(with husks)

4-8 ears of sweet corn
(usually 4 ears to each pot)
Pull off dry outer husks leaving
the inner, clean, pale-green husks
Fold back the green husks
and remove the silks.
Then replace green husks over the ears.
Cut off any excess stalk
Place 4 ears in each pot,
cover and bake for 3 hours.
Serve with butter, olive oil,
salt and pepper, or plain.

My version of a Solar Oven Society recipe.
www.solarovens.org

Basic Beans

2 cups pinto beans
or your favorite type beans
6 cups water
Soak your dry beans overnight.
Rinse and drain.
(I soak my dry beans sometimes
for 3 days or until they start sprouting,
rinsing and draining often.
They cook much faster and are sweeter.)

Add:
1 teaspoon salt
1 teaspoon cumin
½ teaspoon black pepper
1 tablespoon chile powder or red pepper
1 bay leaf (optional)
Cover and cook in solar oven 6-8 hours.

BIG ASS COOKING
(Pork, Beef, and Creamy Dishes)

Pesto Chicken

2 ½ lbs of chicken thighs
or drumsticks
1 ½ lbs of red or
Yukon gold baby potatoes
1 pint of cherry or grape tomatoes
½ cup jarred pesto sauce
2 teaspoons olive oil
Salt and pepper to taste
Bake covered for 3-4 hours
in a 5-quart black pot
or in two 3-quart pots.

Modified from Pesto Chicken Bake recipe
in *Prevention* magazine.

Creamy Spinach Casserole

1 cup milk
1 cup cream
2 cloves
1 bay leaf
1 teaspoon salt
5 slices of precooked ham,
bacon, or chipped beef
(cut into bite-size bits)
3 heaping tablespoons butter
2 cloves chopped garlic
1 cup diced onions
2 tablespoons flour
1 heaping cup grated Gruyere cheese
2 tablespoons lemon zest
1 tablespoon lemon juice
¼ teaspoon black pepper
2 ½ lbs of chopped fresh
or frozen (thawed) spinach

In a mixing bowl or pan combine
all the ingredients except the cheese
and spinach.
In your 5-quart cooking pot place a layer
of spinach then pour some of the milk
mixture over the spinach and sprinkle
a little of the grated cheese.
Continue layering spinach, milk,
and sprinkling of cheese.
Cover and place in your solar oven
for 3-4 hours.

Adapted from a recipe in The Glenwood Gazette

50

Squash Casserole

5 cups yellow squash, fresh,
canned, or frozen
1/2 cup melted butter or oil
1 can cream of chicken soup
2 slices cubed bread
1 cup sour cream
Place squash in your cooking pot
and stir in the remaining ingredients
Cover and cook for 2 ½ to 3 hours

Adapted from the *Crock Pot Cookbook:*
440 Slow Cooker Recipes
by Robert Wilson, Kindle eBook

Barbecue Chicken

1 chicken, cut up and skin removed
1 cup ketchup
3/4 cup brown sugar
3 tablespoons Worcestershire sauce
Place chicken in black cooking pot
Combine remaining ingredients
and pour over chicken
Cover and bake for 4-6 hours

Adapted from the *Crock Pot Cookbook:*
440 Slow Cooker Recipes
by Robert Wilson, Kindle eBook

Breakfast Casserole

32 ounce bag of hash brown potatoes,
thawed
1 pound of ham cut into pieces
1/2 cup diced onions
3/4 pound cheddar cheese diced
1 dozen eggs
1 cup milk
1/2 teaspoon dry mustard
Salt and pepper to taste
Layer the potatoes, ham, onions
and cheese in your 5-quart cooking pot
in two or three layers.
Finish up with cheese
Beat the eggs, milk, mustard,
salt and pepper together
Pour over the whole mixture
Cook for 4-6 hours

Adapted from the *Ultimate Crockpot Cookbook:
750 Slow Cooker Recipes*
by Althea Champlain, Kindle eBook

Solar Baked Florentine

1 1/2 cups cheddar cheese, grated
and divided in half
9 ounce package frozen spinach,
thawed and drained
1 cup white bread, cubed
1 cup fresh button mushrooms, sliced
1/2 cup green onions, thinly sliced
6 eggs
1 1/2 cups milk
1/2 cup heavy cream
1 teaspoon salt
1 teaspoon black pepper
1 teaspoon garlic powder
Layer half of the cheddar cheese,
spinach, bread, mushrooms
and green onions in the bottom
of the cooking pot.

Mix together the eggs, milk, cream,
salt, pepper and garlic powder.
Pour this egg mixture over
the layered mixture. Do not mix.
Sprinkle the remaining cheese on top.
Cover; cook for 3-5 hours.

Adapted from the *Ultimate Crockpot Cookbook:
750 Slow Cooker Recipes* by Althea Champlain,
Kindle eBook

Stuffing

1 1/2 loaves of dried
or toasted bread
2 pieces of celery, diced
1 onion, diced
1 stick of butter, melted
1 can of chicken broth
2 teaspoons salt
1/2 teaspoon pepper
2 teaspoons sage
2 eggs
Cut the bread into pieces.
Mix everything together.
Cover and cook for 3-4 hours

Adapted from the *Ultimate Crockpot Cookbook: 750 Slow Cooker Recipes* by Althea Champlain, Kindle eBook

Hot German Potato Salad

6 cups (30-ounces) sliced raw potatoes
1 cup chopped onion
1 cup chopped celery
1 cup water
1/4 cup cider vinegar
1/4 cup sugar
2 tablespoons tapioca
1/4 teaspoon black pepper
2 teaspoons dried parsley flakes
1/4 cup bacon bits
In your cooking pot, combine potatoes, onions and celery.
In another dish or Ziploc bag, combine water, vinegar, sugar, tapioca, black pepper and parsley flakes.
Pour mixture over potato mixture. Stir.
Cover and cook for 4-6 hours.
Stir in bacon bits. Serve warm.

Adapted from the *Ultimate Crockpot Cookbook: 750 Slow Cooker Recipes* by Althea Champlain, Kindle eBook

Western Omelette Casserole

32 ounces hash browns, thawed
1 pound ham, cubed
1 medium onion diced
1 medium green bell pepper, diced
1 1/2 cups Monterey jack cheese, shredded
12 eggs
1 cup milk
1 teaspoon salt
1 teaspoon black pepper

Place a layer of potatoes on the bottom
of your 5-6 quart cooking pot,
followed by a layer of ham, then onions,
green peppers and cheese.
Repeat the layering process two or three times,
end with a layer of cheese.
Beat the eggs, milk and salt
and pepper together.
Pour over the potato mixture.
Cover and cook for 4-6 hours

Adapted from the *Ultimate Crockpot Cookbook:
750 Slow Cooker Recipes* by Althea Champlain,
Kindle eBook

Spanish Rice

2 pounds ground beef
1 medium onion, diced
1 green pepper, chopped
1 (28-ounce) can stewed tomatoes
1 (16-ounce) can tomato sauce
1 1/2 cups water
2 1/2 teaspoons chile powder (or to taste)
2 teaspoons seasoned salt (to taste)
2 tablespoons Worcestershire sauce
2 cups uncooked rice
3 stalks celery, chopped
Put all ingredients in a 5 quart pot.
Stir thoroughly.
Cover and cook 4-6 hours or all day

Adapted from the *Ultimate Crockpot Cookbook: 750 Slow Cooker Recipes* by Althea Champlain, Kindle eBook

Layered Enchilada Casserole

1 can whole tomatoes
1 small onion, cut into pieces
1 clove garlic, minced
1/2 teaspoon ground red pepper
1/2 teaspoon salt
1 (6-ounce) can tomato paste
1 pound ground beef
2 cup shredded cheddar cheese
9 corn tortillas
Blend tomatoes (undrained),
onion and garlic in blender or food processor,
or chop as small as possible.
Add red pepper, salt and tomato paste. Mix.
Place 3 tortillas in bottom of pot.
Layer on tortillas 1/3 of the ground beef,
1/3 of the sauce and 1/3 of the cheddar.
Repeat layering.
Cover and cook for 4-6 hours.

Adapted from the *Ultimate Crockpot Cookbook:
750 Slow Cooker Recipes* by Althea Champlain,
Kindle eBook

Pork Chops A L'orange

3 pounds pork chops
2 cups orange juice
2 cans mandarin oranges,
drained (11-ounce)
1 can pineapple tidbits,
drained (8-ounce)
Salt and pepper pork chops
and put in cooking pot;
cover with orange juice.
Top with oranges and pineapple
Cover and cook for 4-6 hours.

Adapted from the *Ultimate Crockpot Cookbook:
750 Slow Cooker Recipes* by Althea Champlain,
Kindle eBook

BBQ Chicken

4 lbs boneless and skinless
chicken breasts
3 tablespoons Worcestershire sauce
3 tablespoons vinegar
3 ½ cups (28 ounces) bottled
or homemade barbecue sauce

Place chicken in a 5-quart cooking pot
(or use two 3-quart pots).
Pour barbecue sauce and other ingredients
over the chicken.
Cover and cook for 4-6 hours.

Cheese Strata

6 eggs
24 ounces evaporated milk or cream
1 cup cottage cheese
¾ cup grated Parmesan cheese
3 whole, finely chopped scallions
¼ cup chopped parsley
1 teaspoon salt
1 teaspoon minced rosemary leaves
(or ½ teaspoon dried)
A dash or two of cayenne pepper
Mix all the above together
in a mixing bowl or in your cooking pot.
Then add 8 ounces or so of cubed
sourdough bread
When all the ingredients are in your oiled
or lined cooking pot,
cover and bake for 1 ½ to 2 hours.

Adapted from *Solar Cooking for Home
and Camp* by Linda Frederick Yaffe

Easy Lasagna

1 (30-32 oz) jar of your
favorite spaghetti sauce
½ lb thinly sliced mozzarella cheese
1 pint ricotta or dry cottage cheese
¼ cup grated parmesan cheese
Uncooked lasagna noodles
(enough to fill your pot with 2 layers)
Cover the bottom of your cooking pot
with part of the spaghetti sauce
Spread ricotta on the first layer of noodles
and add half the mozzarella
Add another layer of noodles
and top that with the mozzarella
Top with the remaining sauce,
sprinkle on the grated parmesan
Cover and bake for 3-4 hours.

Adapted from *Eleanor's Solar Cookbook*,
by Eleanor Shimeall

Tex-Mex Lasagna

6 uncooked lasagna noodles
15 ounces canned black beans,
rinsed and drained
1 ½ cups salsa
½ teaspoon ground cumin
4 cloves minced garlic
2 plus ounces of sliced black olives
15 ounces ricotta cheese
1 ½ cups shredded Monterey Jack cheese
16 ounces canned diced tomatoes plus juice
At the bottom of your cooking pot
layer half of all the ingredients,
starting with 3 lasagna noodles.
Repeat layering using the remaining ingredients.
Cover and cook for 5-6 hours

Adapted from *Solar Cooking for Home and Camp*
by Linda Frederick Yaffe

Basic Solar Oven Pasta

Put 2 ½ quarts of water with
a ½ teaspoon salt in a black cooking pot.
Cover and leave in the oven for 2 hours.
Then add and stir in 1 lb of pasta
Cover and put in the oven for 7-20 minutes
depending on type of pasta and type of oven.

Adapted from *Solar Cooking for Home and Camp*
by Linda Frederick Yaffe

SWEET ASS COOKING
(DESSERTS)

Gold Diggers Cake

1 Store Bought Yellow Cake Mix
4 eggs
¾ cup oil or softened butter
One cup water
Mix these together,
then add one can of your favorite frosting
(coconut pecan is good) and mix
Put into a covered skillet or 3-quart pot,
and place in your preheated solar oven
1 hour for a hot sun day
or conventional 350 oven
2 hours for a fall, spring,
or partly cloudy day
2 ½ to 3 hours for winter sun in the south
(Remember don't peek too soon!)

Red Devil Cake

Devil's Food Cake Mix
Can Cherry Pie filling
Package chocolate instant pudding
2 tablespoons vanilla extract
8 oz whipped cream
or whipped topping (if available)

Mix Devil's Food cake according
to the box instructions
Bake in your preheated solar oven
1 hour in full summer sun
(40 min conventional oven)
1 1/2-2 hours fall, spring,
or partly cloudy day
2 ½ hours for southern winter sun

While the cake is still warm,
poke fork holes into it,
Then spread cherry filling over the cake.

While the cake cools prepare pudding
and add vanilla
Then mix the whipped topping into
the pudding and spread over the
cherry filling (omit the whipped topping
if you don't have any,
the cake will still taste great)

Fudgy Pudgy Puddin' Cake

One of Texas Jack's (my gold
prospecting and treasure hunting buddy)
and my favorite recipes was this cake—
until we both had to go on a diet:

1 cup flour
¾ cup sugar
2 tablespoons cocoa powder
2 teaspoons baking powder
½ teaspoon salt
(or use a chocolate cake mix)

½ cup milk
2 tablespoons melted butter
1 teaspoon vanilla

Mix all the above ingredients
in a gallon Ziploc bag
or in your parchment paper
or aluminum foil lined black cooking
pot or pan.

Mix topping ingredients:
¾ cup brown sugar
¼ cup cocoa powder
1 ¾ cups hot water
(heated in solar oven or on stove)
(mix until sugar dissolves,
then pour over unbaked cake)

Bake covered for 1-2 hours

in your pre-heated solar oven or
40 minutes uncovered at 350 degrees
in conventional oven
(Could take 1 ½ to 3 hours
depending on your stove and time of year.)

Serve warm right from the oven!

Cinnamon Apple Crisp
(aka Braying Burro Biscuits)

4-5 cups sliced apples
(peeled or unpeeled)
¾ cup brown sugar
½ cup oats
½ cup flour (white,
unbleached, or whole wheat)
1 teaspoon cinnamon
½ teaspoon nutmeg
1/3 cup softened butter

Smudge a little butter or oil
at the bottom of your lined pot.
Place apples in the bottom of your pot.
Mix the remaining ingredients
and sprinkle it over the apples.

Bake covered 1-2 hours in your solar oven
Could take 1-3 hours
depending on your stove and time of year

Serve warm right from the oven to people,
cool awhile for animal friends.

Lemony Pudding Cake

1 large package (2 layer size)
yellow cake mix
1 package instant lemon pudding
4 eggs
¼ cup oil or softened butter
¾ cup water
1 lemon (if available)
if not add ¼ cup more water

Combine and blend all ingredients
except lemon, in a gallon Ziploc bag,
or in your lightly oiled cooking pot.
Cut and squeeze the lemon into a cup
and pick out the seeds.
Put the juice in the batter and mix.
When the batter is spread in
your cooking pot, sprinkle some
zest of lemon (grated lemon peel)
on top of the batter.

Bake covered in your solar oven for 1-2 hours.
Bake uncovered in conventional oven
at 350 degrees for 45 minutes.

High Noon Cobbler

1 cup flour (white, unbleached,
or organic whole wheat)
1 cup sugar
1 cup milk
1 teaspoon baking powder
½ teaspoon salt
1 egg
½ cup melted butter
1 quart fruit (fruit or berries can be fresh,
frozen, or canned, sweetened
or unsweetened, whatever is available)

Melt the butter in the cooking pan
in the solar oven.
Mix the remaining ingredients (except fruit)
in a gallon Ziploc bag,
Pour into the pan with melted butter
and stir lightly.
Then pour the quart of fruit over the batter.

Bake covered for 1-2 hours.

Turkey Turd Tidbits

(Adapted from Georgia Schumacher's
Lutheran Cook Book)
Originally called Turkey Turd Cookies

½ to ¾ cups sugar
½ to ¾ cups brown sugar
1 cup corn syrup or honey
1 teaspoon vanilla
1 ½ cups (or 16 oz jar) of
crunchy peanut butter
4 cups Rice Krispies

Mix sugars, syrup and vanilla
in a cooking pot
Place pot in preheated solar oven.
Leave it for 1-2 hours.
When the sugars have turned
to a thick syrup,
mix in the peanut butter.
Put the Rice Krispies in a large bowl,
or on parchment paper,
then pour the syrup/peanut butter mixture
on the krispies, stir lightly,
spread on cookie sheet or parchment paper,
let cool and cut into turdlet size.
(This can get messy.)

BIG BUTT BREAD RECIPES

Regular yeast bread cooks best in a solar box oven that reaches 250 to 300 degrees during the mid-day hours. You can use any of your favorite bread recipes and bake the bread in standard dark metal loaf pans or pans painted on the outside with stove black paint. I use my round, black 3-quart pots for all my baking.

Baking powder breads like zucchini bread, beer bread, and banana bread can be baked covered, in any type of solar oven, at lower temperatures, for longer times, without drying out. Because of this, I prefer using baking powder bread recipes. I find yeast breads a pain in the butt.

**Make Three Types of Bread
from One Dough**

Heat 3 cups of water to about 140 degrees
Pour the heated water into
a large mixing bowl
Then add 1 envelope dry yeast
and 1 tablespoon sugar
When the yeast has grown and looks spongy
Add 4 cups flour
4 tablespoons butter or oil
1 teaspoon salt
Mix and add additional flour if necessary
to make it pliable
Set the dough aside in a warm place.
Butter 3 baking pans
(or line with parchment paper)
When the dough is twice its original size,
take about a third of the dough
and shape into small dinner rolls and
place in one of the cooking pots
and set aside to rise.

Put brown sugar and white sugar
(add cardamom, cinnamon or
any spice you want) in the bottom
of another pan.
Take another third of the dough
and roll balls of dough into
this sugar mixture.
Place these sugar-rolled balls
into a cooking pot by layering
and stacking them.

Flatten the last third of dough
into a rectangle shape.
Spread the leftover sugar mixture over
the flattened dough.
Add dabs of butter, jelly, or more sugar
and cinnamon if you want. Roll this into
a log and put it into the remaining pot,
or the roll can be sliced into
cinnamon rolls.

Bake uncovered in a preheated oven,
preferably as close to 300 degrees
as possible, for about 1 hour
or until golden brown.
If your oven is running at a lower
temperature—which happens sometimes
if clouds drift over or the wind picks up—
simply cover the pots
with black lids and cook longer.

Adapted from TheSunWorks.com

Brown Bread

1 egg
1 cup milk
¼ cup brown sugar
2 cups whole wheat flour
1 cup white flour
1 teaspoon baking powder
1 teaspoon baking soda
¼ teaspoon salt
Mix together all the above ingredients
Put the dough on a heavily floured surface
and knead briefly
Form the dough into a loaf
the shape of your cooking pot and
place it in the oiled or parchment lined pot.
Cover and bake in your preheated solar oven
for 3 hours.

Adapted from *Solar Cooking for
Home & Camp* by Linda Frederick Yaffe

Beer Bread

1 ½ cups whole wheat flour
1 ½ cups white flour
¼ teaspoon salt
¼ cup brown sugar
½ teaspoon baking soda
12 ounce bottle of a light lager beer

Mix together all the above ingredients
Spread the dough evenly in an oiled
or parchment lined pot or dark loaf pan
Cover and bake in your preheated oven
for 2 hours
Then using a spatula turn the loaf
upside down, and return it to the
oven uncovered for 1 more hour.

Adapted from *Solar Cooking for
Home & Camp* by Linda Frederick Yaffe

Banana Bread

5 very ripe bananas
2 eggs
½ cup sugar
½ cup oil
2 cups flour
½ teaspoon baking soda
1 teaspoon baking powder
Dash of salt

Mash the bananas,
add the eggs and blend.
Mix in sugar and oil.
Add the remaining dry ingredients
until moist (don't over mix).
Pour into 1 or 2 oiled or
parchment lined baking pots.
Cover and bake for 2-3 hours.

Adapted from TheSunWorks.com

Nut Breads

1 cup whole wheat flour
1¼ cups white flour
3 teaspoons baking powder
½ to ¾ cup sugar
1 teaspoon salt
3 tablespoons oil
1 cup milk
1 egg
½ cup nuts
½ cup sunflower seeds

Mix all the ingredients quickly
Put into a lined or oiled pot
cover, and bake for 2-3 hours

Date or Raisin Bread

Use the above recipe and add
1 cup chopped dates or raisins

Orange Nut Bread

Use the above recipe and add
4 teaspoons orange rind and
replace all or ¾ of the milk
with orange juice

Adapted from *Eleanor's Solar Cookbook*
by Eleanor Shimeall

Zucchini Bread

2 ½ cups flour (white, whole wheat,
or both)
¾ cup sugar
1 egg
2 cups chopped zucchini
1 teaspoon cinnamon
3 teaspoons baking powder
1 teaspoon baking soda
½ cup nuts or sunflower seeds
½ cup oil
½ cup milk
1 teaspoon salt
½ cup raisins

Mix all the ingredients, thoroughly and quickly.
Pour into 1 or 2 oiled or lined baking pots.
Bake for 2-3 hours.

Adapted from *Eleanor's Solar Cookbook*
by Eleanor Shimeall

Chili Corn Bread

2 eggs
¾ cup milk
2 tablespoons oil
¾ cup grated cheddar cheese
4 ounces canned chopped,
hot green chilies, drained
Mix the above ingredients
Then stir in:
1 cup whole wheat flour
½ cup white flour
½ cup cornmeal
1 tablespoon sugar
2 ½ teaspoons baking powder
½ teaspoon salt
Pour the batter into your oiled
or lined pot
Cover and bake for 3 hours

Adapted from *Solar Cooking for
Home & Camp* by Linda Frederick Yaffe

WILD ASS COOKING

Crayfish

Catch 25 to 100 of these tasty little buggers. Leave them in a bucket of clean water overnight. They are cannibalistic so some will get eaten by their bucketmates. In the morning put a quart or two of water into a black cooking pot. Use 2 pots for faster cooking. The amount of water depends on the number of crawdads or crayfish you plan to cook. I like to add ¼ cup salt and chili powder to the water. Salt, bay leaves, peppercorns, and caraway seeds are good also. Place pots of seasoned water into the solar oven. In two or three hours check the steaming water, then dump half the live crayfish into each pot, cover and put back in the solar oven for another hour. Then drain and cool the crayfish and break off the tails and peel, removing the intestinal tract and the bitter gall cyst at the same time.

For Crayfish Cocktail put 5-10 in a cocktail glass or any type of small dish or paper plate and add a dollop of cocktail sauce to each serving.

You can add the cooked crayfish into any soup or gumbo recipe that calls for crab, lobster, or fish.

Hot Crab or Crayfish Dip

8 ounces of softened cream cheese
2 cups plain yogurt or sour cream
4 cloves minced garlic
½ teaspoon salt
¼ teaspoon hot sauce
1 pound flaked crabmeat or crayfish
Stir together in a lined pot and spread
the mixture evenly.
Sprinkle over the top ½ cup
grated Parmesan cheese.
Cover and put in the solar cooker
for 1 hour.
Serve warm with tortilla chips,
crackers, or raw vegetable sticks.

Adapted from *Solar Cooking for
Home and Camp*
by Linda Frederick Yaffe

Pigeon

Years ago a pigeon flock owner, who lived about a mile from me, quit feeding his pigeons. Every morning and evening when I cast bird seed for the Gambel's quail, rock doves, mourning doves, ring neck doves and the many songbirds, these ravenous pigeons descended in groups of 50 or more and gobbled up all the seed in a matter of minutes. I'd finally had enough of feeding the neighbor's birds. I wasn't the only person in the area sick of these birds. So I set traps and shot a few, thinking that they might be as smart as crows and stay away. Nope. They arrived in even larger numbers. So my friend, Texas Jack, an excellent shot, set up his travel trailer near the feeding grounds, opened a window and began picking them off one at a time. At about 75 dead pigeons, the remaining flock moved on to less deadly pastures.

Texas Jack and I are not the type to waste fresh meat. So as the birds were shot either he or I would skin them (I used sharp scissors; he used a sharp pocket knife). I once raised chickens and geese and long since abandoned the ridiculous mess of plucking. Skinning is much more efficient. In a survival situation you may want the skin for the fat, but I let my dogs and cats eat what they wanted of the raw skin and feathers, the rest would go into the crab pot (when I lived on the salt water). At other times when I trapped or shot game birds and lived in a tent or remote cabin, I'd take the skins and feathers away from camp and leave them in the woods or fields where scavengers could get a good meal.

After skinning the pigeons, we removed the breasts and froze them. With a freezer full of breasts, I found a number of recipes that worked well in the solar ovens. To my palate, wild rice or whole grain rice is better with pigeon than potatoes. Pigeon meat is very dark and the older birds are sometimes tough, but they always have a good flavor.

Smothered Pigeon

6-8 pigeon breasts
1 medium or large red or white onion
(sliced or diced)
2-4 tablespoons Worcestershire sauce,
soy sauce or organic liquid aminos
Black pepper
Red pepper and turmeric (optional)
Rice (any type you prefer)
Put 1 cup rice in the bottom of a
lined black pot,
add 2 cups water or broth of your choice.
(A rule of thumb is to cover the rice
with liquid to one inch over.)
Then add ½ the seasoning you wish to use.
Put ½ the onions on top of rice mixture.
Add the pigeon breasts.
Sprinkle on the remaining seasonings
and the rest of the onions.

Bake covered in the solar oven
for 3-6 hours, or all day.

Dove, Rabbit or Pheasant Stew

1 or 2 dressed rabbits or pheasants,
or 8 dove or quail breasts
1 cup sour cream
(you can substitute plain yogurt
or mayonnaise)
1 cup cream of mushroom soup
1/4 teaspoon Worcestershire sauce,
soy sauce, or liquid aminos
2 tablespoons fresh or instant onions
Season meat with salt, pepper, paprika,
and optional red pepper, turmeric
or curry powder
Place meat in the bottom of the lined
or oiled cooking pot
Mix sour cream, soup, Worcestershire sauce,
and onions. Pour this over the meat.
Cook in solar oven 4-5 hours
or all day until you are ready to eat.

This recipe is adapted from the
Ultimate Crockpot Cookbook:
750 Slow Cooker Recipes
by Althea Champlain,
a Smashbooks Kindle Edition.

Baked Dove, Quail, or Pigeon over Christmas Cabbage

1 head of white cabbage,
cored and shredded
½ cup shredded carrots
1 cup whole cranberries
(canned cranberry sauce okay)
1 cup raisins
¼ cup oil or bacon fat
1 medium onion, sliced
½ tablespoon salt
or 1-2 tablespoons soy sauce
½ tablespoon celery salt
1 teaspoon black pepper
1 teaspoon garlic powder
Mix all the above in a lined
cooking pot.

Take breasts of 4 birds and
rub the meat with peanut oil
Place breasts on top of cabbage
Mix a ½ cup of maple syrup with
a little bit of salt, pepper,
garlic powder, and paprika.
Pour this maple syrup mixture
over the bird breasts.
Cover the black cooking pot
and leave in the solar oven
for 2-3 hours.

Adapted from Griswold Inn Recipes

Venison

3-4 pounds venison or any wild meat
1 large onion
16 ounce bottle of cola
24 ounces bottled catsup
Cook in solar oven 4-5 hours
or all day.

Adapted from the *Ultimate Crockpot Cookbook*
by Althea Champlain, a Kindle eBook

Venison Roast

1 venison roast (any cut)
2 cans condensed mushroom soup
1 package dry onion soup mix
1/4 cup red wine (optional)
Mix mushroom soup,
wine and dry soup mix in bottom
of lined black cooking pot.
Place roast on mixture.
Cook in solar oven for 6 hours,
or all day.
Remove roast and slice.
Serve over rice or noodles.

Adapted from the *Ultimate Crockpot Cookbook* by Althea Champlain,
a Kindle eBook

Citrus Fish

1 1/2 pounds fish fillets
1 medium onion, diced
5 tablespoons chopped parsley
4 teaspoons oil or butter
2 teaspoons grated lemon rind
2 teaspoons grated orange rind
Salt or soy sauce
Place fish in bottom of lined black pot,
season to taste.
Put onion, parsley, grated rinds,
and oil over fish.
Cook for 2-3 hours.

Adapted from the *Ultimate Crockpot Cookbook*
by Althea Champlain, a Kindle eBook

Rattlesnake on a bed of rice.

Rattlesnake on a Bed of Rice with onions, garlic, salt, and pepper. Skin and dress one rattlesnake. Cut into steaks or leave whole. I normally cut the snake into steaks, but I leave it whole if I want to discourage dinner guests, or give them something to talk about. Put 1 cup of rice and 2 ½ cups of water or broth into the bottom of a black pot. Cut 1 onion and 2 cloves of garlic and spread over rice. Add salt and pepper. Cajun spices are good with snake also. Place your snake on top of the rice, sprinkle seasoning on the snake. Cover with a black lid and place in the solar oven for 3-6 hours. The longer you leave it the more tender and flavorful the meat.

Ver de Terre

Rewritten from The Peninsula Post column,
"Sows, Cows, and Lots of Bull" by the author

Pickup trucks towing small fishing boats swooshed past my cabin. Some of these trucks stopped in my driveway.

I strategically placed sandwich board signs with big blue arrows and bright red letters. FAT WORMS HERE. The letter "O" in worms is a picture of an earthworm shaped like an O.

I'd seen other signs announcing "We Have Worms!" Were these quarantine warnings for airborne ringworm? Or a public notice of internal parasite infestation? The earthworms painted on my signs cleared up the question "What kind of worms?"

I sell lots of fishing worms to folks with lots of fishing poles stuck in truck cab gun racks. Old men and old women wearing old hokey hats covered with rusty fish hooks, colorful fishing flies, and fish pins and buttons which read, "I'd rather be fishing!" They love my fat worms. I love my fat worms too.

Earthworms smell like fresh clean earth. The large masses of squirming worms feel cool and moist to warm human hands. Counting and sorting worms around here is a high honor.

Worms are useful, harmless and endearing. The name for worm raising in fancy books is vermiculture. Instead of calling ourselves Worm

Farmers we're Vermiculturists. (I still can't pronounce it right.)

Birds dine on juicy worms, fish gobble them up, pigs go to depths to root them out . . . hmm I wondered what they tasted like. My French Canadian relatives serve escargot (snails) alongside clams and oysters. Could worms provide a fine dining experience?

To announce, "Honey, we're having earthworm stir-fry tonight," would not work. I never say "I had snails for lunch," but instead "I ate escargot." I say, "The Calamari was seasoned perfectly," instead of "Hey, great squid!" Oh! Worm of the soil. "Ver de Terre." Humble beast! Yum yum!

Ver de Terre, like escargot, must first be washed and soaked in cold water. If these are worms raised in livestock manure, like mine are, I simply put a large number of the fattest worms in my compost heap of coffee grounds, cornmeal, and wet newspapers for a few days. Then I boiled them lightly to remove bits of soil. To do this in a solar oven use the same method as cooking crayfish, except less time is needed. Then I dry them by putting a board or rack in the cooking area of the solar oven (no pot or cooking bag is needed), spread out parchment paper (secure it if it is breezy), on cheesecloth, or cotton cloth, then spread out a layer of worms (or anything you want to dry), sprinkle with salt and pepper or any of your favorite seasonings, or sugar for dessert toppings. Position the solar oven toward the sun and in a few hours they will be dried to perfection and ready to add to any dish. Who needs croutons!

Ver de Terre are entirely edible, with no bones or gristle to throw away! The subtle chestnut flavor of Ver de Terre lends itself well to all sorts of ingredients and methods of preparation. I've tried "Caesar Salada au Ver de Terre," (using dried and crumbled Ver de Terre instead of bacon bits.) We can't forget, "Canapes Ver de Terre," and "Consomme Ver de Terre.

When you serve a Ver de Terre dish you will impress your family and friends (as I have) with your sense of adventure and worldliness. "Ver de Terre au Fromage Suisse" (baked Ver de Terre mixed with a sauce of melted Swiss cheese), a favorite at cocktail parties. Lightly salted, butter-fried Ver de Terre takes the place of shoestring potatoes and Chow Mein noodles, and is a crunchy hit at outdoor barbecues. Add them to a Nut Bread recipe, and call it your Nut Bread Surprise. Perfect for church bake sales.

BAD ASS SURVIVAL FOOD

Whether it's a natural disaster or you lose your job, you may, temporarily, find yourself living in a tent, a cave, or in your car.

For 4-8 months per year (totaling about 15 years) I lived in a tent or mine shack—usually at mine sites in remote areas of Alaska, Idaho, New Mexico, and Colorado. I even spent a few summers in an underground mine tunnel. Sometimes roads washed out, bridges collapsed, and rivers flooded, leaving no access to the outside world and basic food for sometimes months at a time. So I lived off the land and fed my dogs and cats. Under extreme circumstances even strict vegetarians will eat fish, tadpoles, crickets, mice, and rats or anything to keep up their strength to survive. The addition of a solar oven or two in your survival gear, can make a difficult situation easier.

Mice and rats are mainly dark meat and taste a lot like squirrel. Mice and rats from the forest and meadow are not like the mud-flavored, garbage eating, city rodents. They are not much different than eating a squirrel or rabbit, and easier to catch. You may cringe at this prospect right now, but keep it in mind when you and your pets get really hungry, rodents are available year round.

My favorite insects to cook and eat are grasshoppers and any large grubs. Grubs are best baked with lots of seasoning and vegetables (if available). Grasshoppers are good dried or baked, with or without legs and wings. If you haven't poisoned your lawn you can have nice salad greens from your dandelions too!

A fun book is *The Eat-A-Bug Cookbook* by David George Gordon (author of *The Compleat Cockroach*). It's full of recipes for succulent items like, "Tantalizing Termites (The Other White Meat)". This bug book is a great introduction to the world of edible insects. In a survival situation you won't be having a Three Bee Salad (pupae, larvae, and adult bees) or Cream of Katydid Soup, but you can roast or boil the protein packed morsels. The only cautions are: don't eat vividly colored bugs, as they are often poisonous; and cook your edible bugs if possible. After reading this bug cookbook you will never look at a cockroach in the same way.

I recommend keeping on hand, books about the edible and medicinal plants of your home base region and the places you frequent. Getting stranded and running out of food can become a challenging adventure instead of a fear driven nightmare.

A solar oven in your emergency pack can be used on any sunny day to sterilize water and dry food.

Smart Ass Guide to Solar Food Drying & Water Purifying

Food Drying

During the warm, dry season I've successfully dried meat, fruit, and vegetables on a tin roof (never do this on an asphalt roof) by laying down a cotton sheet and anchoring it with bricks or rocks. Then, for example, I'd lay my thin strips of meat on the sheet, then cover with another cotton sheet or cheese cloth. Leave the meat for one day then turn the meat strips over the second day. By the second evening the meat should be dried and ready to store.

If I have fruit, vegetables, and meat to process, and I have to use the same cloth for the drying process, I start by processing the fruit, followed by the vegetables, then the meat. If you are drying fish, always do the fish last or have a separate area, cloth or mesh for fish only.

Besides a tin roof, another good place to dry food is in a tent, also during the warm, dry season. Tables or racks can be put in the tent and you can process an entire winter's supply of food. Tent drying does not require you to cover the food with a cotton sheet or cheesecloth. Flies won't get in and the tent itself will provide some shade from direct sun. Direct sun can bleach the food and zap some of the nutrients. Whatever tent or tents you use for food processing should never be used for camping in, as the aromatic tent will act as a lure for hungry critters.

I met a guy who used the interior of his car to dry food and herbs. He set up oven racks, stacked five high, in his back seat. He left the front windows cracked about a half inch or so, and left the vehicle in the sun. He didn't put any kind of cover on his drying food. Anyone who lives in a sunny climate, knows all to well, that an automobile is a large solar oven. Try sitting on that dark blue, vinyl seat in shorts.

The fold-up and funnel ovens pictured at the beginning of this book are perfect for solar drying on a small scale. First I lay down two or three layers of cotton fabric on the flat, cooking surface, where I normally place my cooking pots. You can also use a flat piece of wood, covered with cheese cloth or cotton fabric. Pillow cases are a perfect size. I get a few dozen cotton pillowcases every year from a thrift shop or rummage sale and launder them, sometimes twice, without detergent, and dry them on high heat, turned inside out, without any dryer sheets.

Though some people do, I never blanch or put sulfur on my fruit or vegetables. When I hand collect edibles in the forest, like rose hips or huckleberries, I don't bother washing them before drying. I do wash fruits and veggies such as apples and potatoes.

Slice meat, vegetables, and fruit into long thin slices for faster drying. If you don't like the way sliced apples and pears turn brown, sprinkle sugar or cinnamon, or both, on the fruit. When processing meat, if you are having problems with flies and yellow jackets, sprinkle the thinly sliced meat on both sides with black pepper.

Lay your thinly sliced food close together, but not touching, filling the flat, cooking area of your solar oven. Cover with a piece of cloth and let dry in the open, heated air. The sliced food will normally shrink to half its size during the drying process. You can turn your drying food half way through the first day, or turn it over the following day. By the end of the first day some thinly sliced veggies will be dry enough to store for future use.

Vegetables should be rattle-dry. Fruit and tomatoes are done when leathery. In the evening when the air cools and becomes moist, you should roll your drying food in the cloth it is laying on and store it in a safe place indoors. I use 18-gallon plastic bins with tight lids or 5-gallon white plastic buckets with tight lids. White buckets are best because they are often used for food. Don't store your drying or dried food in black plastic garbage bins. They smell strongly of plastic and can ruin your carefully dried food.

Depending on your location and time of year, drying should take no more than 2 or 3 days. Some people prefer their dried meat leather dry; I prefer mine rattle dry. That way I never have to deal with mold. The dogs enjoy dried sweet potatoes and dried liver strips. The cats like dried liver cut into small pieces.

The best way to store your dried food is to place it in paper lunch sacks, then put the filled sacks into gallon Ziploc bags. On the outside, mark the date and contents. Store for up to a year in odor free bins.

Sun Crackers

1 cup whole wheat flour
1 cup white flour
2 tablespoons wheat germ
1/3 cup vegetable oil
(part sesame oil is good)
1 tablespoon soy sauce
1/3 cup sesame seeds
1 teaspoon molasses
Mix all the ingredients
Add sprinkling of water as needed
Spread dough on floured cookie sheet
and roll as thin as possible
Cut into squares and leave
on the cookie sheet
Place the cookie sheet in the
open solar oven.
Do not cover.
Check for crispness in 2 or 3 hours.

Adapted from *Solar Cooking,*
A Primer/Cookbook by Harriet Kofalk

Wholesome Crackers

¾ cup whole wheat flour
¼ cup white flour
1 teaspoon oat or wheat bran
1 tablespoon brown sugar
¾ teaspoon baking powder
¼ teaspoon salt
¼ cup cold butter
Mix all the above ingredients
together except the butter
Cut in the butter a little at a time.
When the dough forms balls
sprinkle in a few tablespoons cold water
Knead the dough for 20 or 30 seconds,
put on a floured board
Roll the dough as thin as possible
Slice into 1 or so inch rectangles.
Punch holes with a fork
so they don't buckle
Put them at the bottom of
black cooking pots
or on an oiled, dark cookie sheet
Place them uncovered in your oven's
cooking area.
Turn the crackers in 2 hours,
and let them dry and bake another hour.

Adapted from *Solar Cooking for Home
& Camp* by Linda Frederick Yaffe

Water Purifying

Your solar oven can pasteurize water. When water is heated to 150 degrees for 10 minutes it is pasteurized. (At 160 degrees for 10 minutes, milk and food is pasteurized). 150 degrees kills fecal contaminants like E. coli; giardia cysts; and viruses like rotavirus, enterovirus, and hepatitis A. In a solar oven this may take 60 to 90 minutes per quart.

Do this by putting untreated water in black pots or black jars in your solar box oven. Put the water containers in a roasting bag if you are using an open oven. Leave for at least an hour. With clean hands check if water is hot enough by using an instant-read thermometer, or check if the water is boiling. SolarOvens.org sells a Water Pasteurization Indicator referred to as the WAPI. This is a simple, small thermometer containing wax that melts at 156 degrees, which means the water has been 150 degrees for more than ten minutes and is sterilized. The Solar Oven Society provides a WAPI with each solar oven it sells.

Knowing this might come in handy during natural disasters and long power outages. Note: Water sterilizing will not filter out or remove any chemical or metal contaminants.

Desperate Ass
(Ingredient Substitutions)

Slow, crock-pot style cooking does not require the precision necessary for gourmet dishes. So be flexible about substituting ingredients.

If you run out of eggs, use mayonnaise, or baking powder and water, or a dash of baking powder in plain yogurt, sour cream, or cottage cheese. A medium egg is about 2 ounces or 5 tablespoons of liquid.

If you run out of sugar use honey or syrup in the same quantity, cup for cup. Then reduce the amount of liquid.

To make buttermilk substitute, use 1 tablespoon of vinegar or lemon juice per cup of milk, and let stand for about 5 minutes. Or an equal amount of plain yogurt.

If you are out of fresh milk use powdered milk or use a ½ portion of evaporated milk with a ½ portion of water. Or use the same amount of water, fruit juice, vegetable juice or any liquid compatible with your recipe.

1 cup vegetable shortening is equal to 7/8 cup lard or oil, and equal to 1 1/8 cups butter or margarine.

½ tablespoon cornstarch is equal to 1 tablespoon of flour.

1 cup whole or white flour is equal to ¾ cup cornmeal or 1 ½ cups ground rolled oats.

1 heaping tablespoon is 2 level tablespoons.

1 teaspoon allspice is close to ½ teaspoon cinnamon and ½ teaspoon ground cloves.

1 teaspoon baking powder is equal to ¼ teaspoon baking soda plus 5/8 teaspoon cream of tartar. I rarely have cream of tartar on hand, so when I'm out of baking powder I use ½ the amount of baking soda. There is no substitute for baking soda.

1 cup cream equals ¾ cup milk plus ¼ cup butter.

For an extensive list of ingredient substitutions go to:
AllRecipes.com/HowTo/Common-Substitutions/
Detail.aspx

Cornbread & Beans

Story reprinted from *Gold Prospectors
Magazine* and *Desert Exposure* Magazine

The morning sun warms the reddish coarse sand speckled with pyrite where I toss my nylon tent. Anne Marie, my cat, tunnels under the fabric, and Joey the dog flops near the tunneling cat bulge, rolls onto his back and wriggles side to side like a beached fish. I watch laughing, hands on my hips. "Dang you guys, how will I ever get our tent up!"

My pack donkeys, Shaggy and Willy, ten feet away behind their solar-charged polywire corral, eye the rippling fabric, hoping for a chance to play tug-of-war. For now they'll have to make do tugging on sticks; my tent is off limits.

I planned this weeklong trip of blissful solitude to the Steeple Rock Mining District east of the Arizona state line in search of mineral and rock pigments: the red oxide of hematite; the shades of yellow, ochre, sienna, and umber found in limonite; azurite blues, and malachite greens. When I mentioned to some artist friends in Silver City about painting landscapes using natural pigments found locally, they offered to buy every pigment I could dig up.

I lure the dog and cat away with liver treats and set the tent up, then I put the solar oven on a folding table in the sun on this April day under an infinite blue sky. I line two black roasting pans with aluminum foil (to save water and scrubbing), then squeeze half of the stiff premixed cornbread batter from the gallon Ziploc bag into each pot. To one pan of batter I stir in some olive oil and a can of drained corn and teaspoon of salt—this one to accompany the beans; to the other pot I add safflower oil, two eggs, and quarter cup of brown sugar—a breakfast cornbread. The cornbread will bake to perfection in two hours; three hours if scattered clouds move in.

I drain the red beans I've been soaking for two days, add fresh water to the two-gallon bean pot, and turn it to low simmer on the two-burner propane stove. I'll add spices after I unpack the rest of my kitchen.

A few hours later I hear a vehicle and see dust rise from the road below me. I'm far enough off the dipping and hair-pinning dirt road that travelers shouldn't notice me, I hope.

Then I see Texas Jack's faded gray Jeep Cherokee slow, stop, back-up about fifteen feet, then turn into my tracks. One hundred feet behind him is a late model Chevy truck with an expensive looking overhead camper. As the Jeep gets closer I see curious cat faces pressed against the back-seat window.

I thought Texas Jack was checking out mining claims in the Santa Rita Mountains with some guy called Gerald the Joker—reputably not a humorist but a card shark.

After Texas Jack parks and climbs out of his Jeep I ask, "Why are you here? Did somebody die?"

He smiles, "Makin' sure you got camped okay. He—" Texas Jack gestures toward the truck that is now backing in, "wanted to stop and say howdy on our way."

"Oh." I turn, then look back at him, "I left a voicemail telling you where I was for an emergency; it wasn't an invitation." I walk away to stir my beans.

117

He opens the Jeep's rear door and three cats jump out and make a dash to my tent, start climbing, wrestling, and chasing Joey and Anne Marie. The animal antics make me laugh. The donkeys watch, curious for awhile, then resume munching the dry tufted ricegrass.

We make introductions. Gerald the Joker is a big soft man, maybe six-feet-five, with pale baby hair, fish-pale eyes, and large pink hands. In contrast, his wife is about five-feet tall, desert tortoise skin stretched tight over angular bones, a startling contrast to her chrome blue eyes framed in a well-cut pageboy of shiny auburn hair. She doesn't smile.

The aroma of baking cornbread floats through camp. My stomach growls.

Texas Jack says, "Something smells right good. Too bad we can't stay, gotta get goin' soon."

Gerald the Joker laughs, "Hell, I'm in no hurry, I'm retired." He slaps me on the back and says, "Ole Texas Jack says you make a mean red bean soup. Sounds good to me, but I don't like onions."

I packed a week's worth of food for myself and my critters. I expected the beans and cornbread to last me three or four days.

I continue cooking the beans, adding four cans of tomato paste; two cans diced tomatoes; three diced eye burning purple onions—snickering to myself about 'but I don't like onions'—yeh, but I do. Then I add a heaping eighth-cup of hot green chile powder, and a heaping eighth-cup of hot red chile powder. I smile to myself, whistling a verse from "Don't Fence Me In."

I hear clattering and Gerald the Joker talking. I turn to look and Mrs. Joker is unfolding two yellow lawn chairs. Texas Jack is perched on his beat-up metal folding chair.

The three guests now seated face the fifty-mile view of rugged peaks, mesas, rust red, purple and pink canyons with iron streaked tailing dumps, and sharp silhouettes of soaptree yuccas; the scene softened by weathered hills veiled in the wispy lime and avocado greens of Gambel oak, cherrystone juniper, and Apache and piñon pine.

"Hey, Jill," I hear Gerald the Joker call, "any chance for some of your famous bad ass coffee?"

Looking at the back of his head I call back, "Don't you guys have coffee in your rig?"

"Yeh, but travlin' and all, everything is packed, got boxes strapped on top of the stove."

"Sorry, just rinsed the pot out, can't spare the drinking water."

Then he adds, "Maybe tomorrow morning then."

"Tomorrow morning? I thought you guys were on a mining claim mission?"

No one answers my question.

The baby haired man looks at his wife, "Woman! Get me a cold diet Coke from the cooler, the red cooler with ice, under the table."

Mrs. Joker rises slowly, she adjusts the steps then climbs into the camper, moves some boxes around; I hear a lid squeak, and she comes out, two cans dripping. Hers is a root beer.

"Thanks for the offer," I mumble to myself. I look at the back of Texas Jack's head, he is talking about a lost gold ledge in the Santa Rita Mountains.

As an afterthought I decide to add ten jalapeño peppers to the beans, seeds and all; burns going down, and if you are afflicted with hemorrhoids burns like the fire of hell going out, so I'm told.

The beans bubble, releasing the smell of roasted green chile and the nutty sweet smell of beans.

I haul water to the donkeys from the five-gallon cans in my truck bed, use my makeshift privy with camo curtain, grab the toilet paper and stash it in my tent just for spite, then call the cats and dog into the tent and zip it up so I can eat in peace, wash my hands in the dish water, go back to the bean pot, stir and check the beans for softness and say, "Soup's on. Find yourself a bowl and spoon. I only have one spoon and one chipped enamel bowl," I lie.

Again he orders his wife, "Get me that big ceramic bowl, the blue one, and a big spoon." He turns his head slightly and looks at me with one eye, "Is the cornbread done?"

"Maybe."

"Woman. Grab me a plate, knife, and the tub of butter. How about a TV tray too."

When I glance into the open camper door, I see the glint of a large knife that Mrs. Joker lifts and looks at for a moment, then slowly puts down. She pauses, then gathers the plates, TV tray, and silverware.

I cut the steaming cornbread into four pie shaped hunks. I'm not concerned with hospitality, so I plunk my cornbread in the bottom of my bowl and ladle the bean soup over it. I walk to my lawn chair and sit. My guests remain seated, waiting. With my spoon I motion for them to get up and fill their own bowls and plates.

Texas Jack says, "Where's my bowl?"

"Gee, I don't know? Where is your bowl?"

Laughing, he pushes himself up and says, "Just kidding," goes to his Jeep and rummages around and comes up with a mess-kit pan and silverware.

I put a big spoonful of beans in my mouth. I almost gasp. This is hot, hot, hot. Whoa. But I keep a straight face. After a few more bites my taste buds adjust and relax. Hmm, tastes pretty good.

I watch while Mrs. J puts the cornbread on Baby Hair's plate, lathers it an inch high with margarine, expressionless she brings it to him. He says, "I need another Coke after you get my beans." Then I watch while she ladles the beans into his ceramic bowl.

She moves slowly to the camper and delivers another dripping soda. "You forgot the napkins." She trudges back to the camper for napkins. Meanwhile Texas Jack is loading his pan with cornbread and beans. Texas Jack likes spicy food almost as much as I do. After Baby Hair is served and napkined, Mrs. J gets her cornbread and beans in a kid-size plastic bowl.

Then I hear the roar. "I said no onions!"

I calmly remark to the back of his head, "Just pick them out—"

I'm interrupted by gasping. "You're trying to kill me!"

Obviously the delayed sting of the jalapeños hit his lips, tongue, and throat. He chokes, coughs like he's about to dislodge all his innards, struggles for air and turns his head toward me, his eyes are popped out like in a cartoon. By then I'm laughing so hard my eyes are running and I've got to stop so I don't pee my pants. I blow my nose and cough. He mistakes my tears and chokes of laughter for shared pain.

He rasps, "You can't even eat your own food." Then he chokes out the words, "I need more cornbread, another soda. Quickly, quickly!"

With insincere sweetness I say, "I'm so, so sorry. I accidentally dropped the other pan of cornbread, the donkeys are eating it now." Another lie, the cornbread is safe on the floorboard of my truck. I stashed it while everyone was admiring the scenery.

Mrs. J gets up, puts her plate on her chair and her root beer on the ground next to her chair. She turns, looks at me, grins with perfect white teeth, but her conspiratorial smile disappears when he tells her to hurry.

After our memorable late lunch I gather two five-gallon buckets with digging tools and Ziploc bags for specimens. While the men are talking I leave unnoticed, followed by the cats and dog, into the purple and red canyon behind camp. Anne Marie my tabby reluctantly acts as Pied Piper to Texas Jack's young cats. She turns, hisses, and swats at them. I imagine she is asking the energetic cats to go home. "Anne Marie, I know exactly how you feel."

I dig samples from weathered deposits of deep red oxides and rich yellow ochres and watch the cats and dog chasing and pouncing on each other under a pyramid shaped Arizona cypress. As I look in the wash I see oxidized azurite float and follow it into a side canyon thick with alligator juniper and piñon pine.

The cats follow behind me, dashing from cover to cover. At the end of this narrowing side canyon is a banded rhyolite wall thrust conspicuously into the maze of crumbling mineralized deposits in massive purple and green andesite. I'm ready to turn back when Joey races by and disappears behind the rhyolite wall. The cats zip past. I follow taking a hard left turn, dragging and scraping my buckets on the rock wall, then a right turn into a three-foot to four-foot wide trail with ankle to knee-high blue, green, and chalcopyrite rocks. Joey runs back to me scrabbling over and around the colorful copper ore boulders, and I notice his feet are covered in red mud.

This bucket scraping trail opens into a sixty-foot by one-hundred-fifty-foot box canyon with rice, fluff and needle grasses flowing around silverleaf oak, and a cluster of Arizona ponderosa pines; on my right Fremont cottonwoods with new spring leaves grow along a vertical wall. The canyon wrens, pine jays, and sage sparrows stop singing, flit for cover, and watch the cats. A few minutes later the canyon birds resume their songs.

Joey's red mud footprints lead to a cleft in the wall behind the cottonwoods. I look up and see green algae with clear water dribbling into a

123

washtub size shelf basin. The overflow seeps into the red clay at my feet.

Hmm, I think to myself, I might move camp here after everyone leaves. If I remove the donkeys' panniers before the first tight turn they should squeeze through. I will tell Texas Jack about this happy valley, but not now.

The next morning I sit in my lawn chair next to Texas Jack. We look at the scenery and sip my fresh boiled Italian roast coffee.

Then I hear bellowing and cursing coming from my curtained-off privy hole. Gerald the Joker is yelling, "Where is the toilet paper!" More moans and bellowing.

I comment to Texas Jack, "Sounds like he has hemorrhoids the size of pomegranates."

Meanwhile I notice out of the corner of my eye Mrs. J moving in slow motion putting one yellow lawn chair in the back of the camper. A bit curious I watch her lock the camper door, and without a glance back she climbs into the truck, slides the seat forward, cranks the engine, releases the emergency brake, rolls over the bumpy track, and turns left onto the gravel road. The gravel crunches and pings, leaving a low drifting dust cloud. Texas Jack and I watch silently. A single yellow lawn chair faces the view.

Then more yelling from the outhouse area, "What the hell is going on out there?"

Choking with laughter I yell back, "I think your wife went to town to get toilet paper!"

Texas Jack with his coffee cup in hand gets up and walks toward the road; he stops, and watches as the dust trail fades.

Pomegranate Buns yells something about bringing him some toilet paper, I yell back between gasps of laughter, "Use your underwear!" I hear more cursing.

Texas Jack returns, "Yep, she's gone."

"Yep, and it's time for you to take Pomegranate Buns home. I'll see you in a week or two."

I'm anxious to pack the donkeys and move to the little oasis Joey found, do some test panning for gold, and see if any well-formed crystals are hidden in the oxidized azurite before I pulverize it for paint pigment. If I run out of food I'll take a half day and go to town. The little drama of Pomegranate Buns's wife driving off into the lavender morning was well worth the brief inconvenience.

The End

About the Author

Laura Leveque aka Jackass Jill, is a freelance outdoor writer and western artist.

She earned a BA from Washington State University and an MA from Central Washington State University.

Leveque gold mined in Alaska, Idaho, Washington, and New Mexico, and has treasure hunted in most western states. She also worked as an underground mine tour guide and donkey packer in Colorado and New Mexico.

She's written travel and adventure stories for publications such as: *Peninsula Post, RV'n Magazine, Gold and Treasure Hunter* magazine, *Southwest On-line* magazine, *Harness Goat Society News*, Sussex, England, *Women and Guns* magazine, and more.

Laura wrote the "Donkey Prospector" column for *Gold Prospectors* magazine and *The Brayer* magazine from 1996 to 2011. In 2011 she began writing the "Treasure Tales and Trails" column for *Gold Prospectors* magazine.

Jackass Jill and Shaggy

Other Books and Publications by Laura Leveque

Whoa you Donkey . . . Whoa! 2006 (paperback), Kindle e-book 2011

Dead Men Drift, An Underground Mine Adventure 2006 screenplay

Donkey Packing Basics, 2011 Kindle e-book

Raise Red Worms, 2011 Kindle e-book

Traveling & Camping With Pets (Dogs, Cats, & Donkeys), 2012 Kindle e-book

Adventures with Ghosts & Spirits, 2012 Kindle e-book

The Silver Bell Mine—Edgar the Pet Rat's Adventures—Five Short Animal & Ghost Stories 2012 Kindle e-book

Hail the Camp! Silver Dollars & Shadowgees, 2014 Kindle e-book

Plus three out-of-print books, written in the 1990s

And more.

Made in the USA
San Bernardino, CA
12 November 2015